Lives and Times

George Eastman

Jennifer Blizin Gillis

Heinemann Library
Chicago, Illinois

Page layout by Cherylyn Bredemann
Photo research by Bill Broyles

Printed and bound in Hong Kong and China by South
China Printing Co Ltd

08 07 06 05 04
10 9 8 7 6 5 4 3 2 1

**Library of Congress
Cataloging-in-Publication Data**
George Eastman / Jennifer Blizin Gillis.
ISBN 1-4034-5326-8 (HC), 1-4034-5334-9 (Pbk.)
The Cataloging-in-Publication Data for this title is on
file with the Library of Congress.

Acknowledgments
The author and publishers are grateful to the following
for permission to reproduce copyright material:
Title page, icons Heinemann Library; pp. 4, 9, 11, 12, 13,
14, 15, 17, 18, 19, 21, 23, 27, 29 George Eastman
House, Rochester, NY; p. 5 The Advertising
Archive/Picture Desk; p. 6 Rare Books Digital/Visual
Resources Librarian, University of Rochester; pp. 7, 20
Lee Snider/Corbis; pp. 8, 24 Bettmann/Corbis; p. 10
Hulton Archive/Getty Images; p. 16 Hartman Center for
Sales, Advertising and Marketing History/Duke
University; p. 22 Underwood & Underwood/Corbis; p. 25
Dennis Szeba/George Eastman House, Rochester, NY;
p. 26 James Lemass/Index Stock Imagery; p. 28 Albert J.
Blodgett/George Eastman House, Rochester, NY

Cover photographs by (top left, bottom left) Heinemann
Library, (bottom right) George Eastman House,
Rochester, NY

The publisher would like to thank Charly Rimsa for her
comments in the preparation of this book.

Every effort has been made to contact copyright
holders of any material reproduced in this book. Any
omissions will be rectified in subsequent printings if
notice is given to the publisher.

Some words are shown in bold, **like this.**
You can find out what they mean by
looking in the glossary.

Contents

A Snapshot of George Eastman

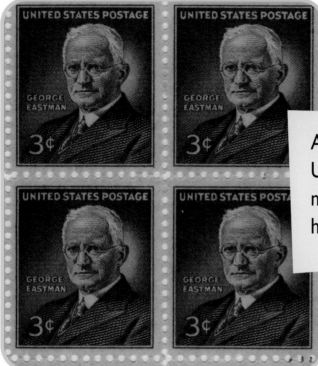

After George died, the United States Post Office made this stamp to honor him.

George Eastman did not invent **photography.** But his inventions made photography fun and easy. George made it possible for anyone to own and use a camera.

George's company had a saying. It was, "You press the button, we do the rest."

George's company was the first to make cameras small enough to hold in your hands. His company's cameras were easy for everyone to use.

Early Life

George was born in Waterville, New York, in 1854. When he was six years old, his family moved to Rochester. His father started a school for people who wanted to work as secretaries and **bookkeepers.**

George was about three years old when this picture was taken.

George lived in this house until he was six years old.

Just before George turned eight, his father died. George's mother opened a **boarding house** to earn money for the family. When he was old enough, George got a job to help earn extra money.

First Jobs

George went to work as a **messenger.** He made $3 a week. That is about $38 in today's money. In his free time, he studied to be a **bookkeeper.**

At his first job, George ran errands, swept the floor, and kept the **woodstove** going in cold weather.

George first became interested in photography while he was working at this bank.

When he was nineteen, George went to work at the Rochester Savings Bank. Soon, he became an assistant bookkeeper. He made $1,000 per year. In 1874 that was a good amount of money.

Photography

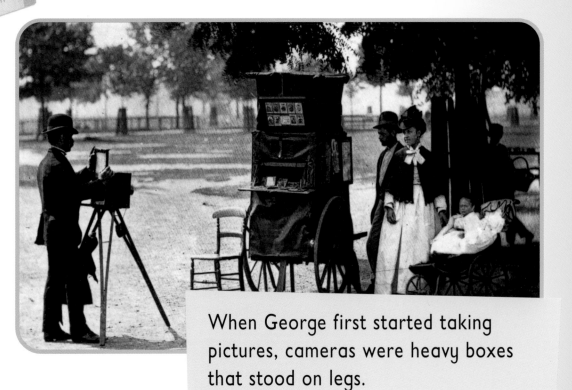

When George first started taking pictures, cameras were heavy boxes that stood on legs.

George bought his first camera to take on vacation. Cameras then were big and heavy. Pictures were taken on glass **plates.** George had to buy **chemicals** to make plates for each picture.

George got more interested in **photography.** He read about something called "dry plates." They were made with the chemicals already on them. He started making them in his mother's kitchen.

This is the first picture George ever took with his camera.

New Company

George invented a machine to put **chemicals** on the dry **plates.** Now, he would not have to add the chemicals by hand. He started the Eastman Dry Plate Company in 1881.

A family friend gave George some of the money he needed to start his company.

This photograph was made using George's dry plates.

George hired someone to make the dry plates. Then, George quit his job at the bank. Many other companies made **photography** supplies. George knew he would have to work hard make his company stand out.

Pictures on a Roll

Photographers put a roll of film in the camera using a holder like this. The photographer had to roll the film to the next **frame.**

George looked for a way to take pictures without glass **plates.** He **experimented** with covering long rolls of paper with **chemicals.** Then, he and a partner invented a holder for the film.

Only a few photographers used George's film and its holder. George decided to make **photography** popular with everyday people. George thought people would buy cameras if they were easier to use.

When this picture of George was taken, it was very unusual for families to own their own cameras.

The Kodak Moment

In 1888 George's company began to sell cameras that fit in people's hands. He used **advertising** to sell his film and cameras. He put advertisements in newspapers, magazines, and on buildings.

Kodak advertisements often had beautiful drawings like this.

n again, when snow and ice hold all out-doors—

KODAK

Turn the lens into the home and picture, for the days to come, its hearthstone harmonies. The album of baby and the pictures made by the little folks will be held more precious every year.

And picture making is easy now—the Kodak has made it so. No dark-room, few chemicals, no fuss. It's photography with the bother left out.

BROWNIE CAMERAS, they work like Kodaks, KODAKS.

$1.00 to $9.00
$5.00 to $100.00

Catalogue, free at the dealers.

EASTMAN KODAK CO.

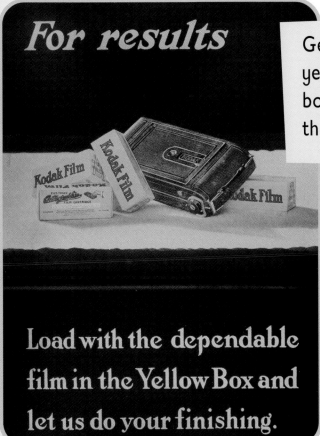

For results

George chose a bright yellow color for his film boxes. The color is still the same today.

Load with the dependable film in the Yellow Box and let us do your finishing.

Today, the name *Kodak* is known all over the world. But the name was one of George's inventions, too! George liked the sound of the letter *k*. He thought people would like the name *Kodak* cameras.

The Click of a Button

George's new cameras were popular.
To take a picture, people just pushed a
button. They could take 100 pictures with
one roll of film. But the camera cost $25.
That is almost $400 in today's money!

When people finished a
roll of film, they sent the
whole camera back to
Kodak with the film
inside. The company sent
back the pictures and the
camera with a new roll
of film inside it.

George told his workers that they needed to make a smaller, cheaper camera. In 1900 Kodak started selling Brownie cameras. Each one cost $1. These cameras were very popular.

Brownie camera boxes were decorated with cartoon characters, so they were popular with children.

A New House and a Sad Time

By 1902 George had made a lot of money. He built a **mansion.** The new house had a **laboratory,** a music room, and a room where George and his friends could watch movies.

Outside, George's house had vegetable and flower gardens, a lily pond, and **orchards.**

After George's mother broke her hip, she used a wheelchair.

George never married. He lived with his mother all his life. But in 1904 she broke her hip. Then, she got very sick. In 1907 George's mother died. He was very sad.

A Good Boss

When George's company made extra money, George shared it with his workers.

George worked almost all the time. He made his workers work hard, too. But he was a fair boss. When workers had ideas that would help the company, George gave them money.

If his workers got hurt, George made sure they had money for doctors. When they got too old to work, George made sure they had money to buy food and clothes.

This picture of George was taken on a visit to France in 1890.

Hobbies

As George's company became more successful, he spent more time doing things he enjoyed. George liked to travel. He also liked to make things with wood.

George traveled to Africa. This picture shows him (on the right) with a friend.

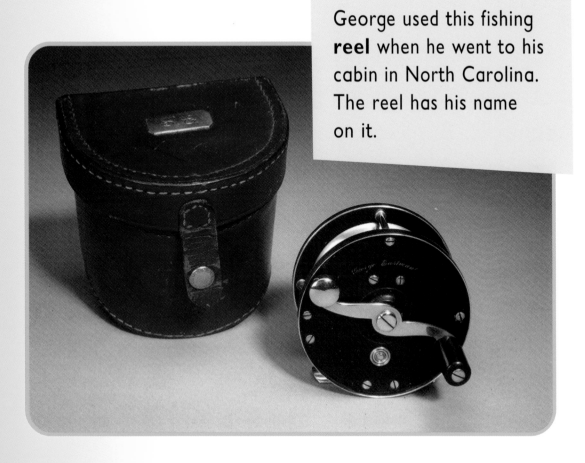

George used this fishing **reel** when he went to his cabin in North Carolina. The reel has his name on it.

George also had a cabin in the mountains of North Carolina. He liked to go there with his friends to hunt and fish. He was a very good cook. He was often in charge of the food on these trips.

Gift-Giver

George believed in sharing his money with others. He gave millions of dollars to schools. But George did not like people to know that he was giving them money. Sometimes he used a different name.

George gave $20 million to this college in Massachusetts. But he told the school the money came from someone named Mr. Smith.

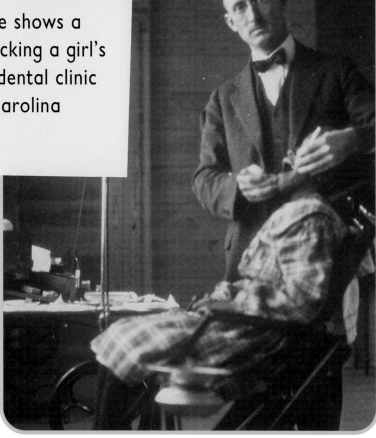

This picture shows a dentist checking a girl's teeth in a dental clinic in North Carolina in 1921.

George knew that many children did not have money to go to the dentist. He started **dental clinics** for children in Rochester, New York, and other towns.

Slowing Down

In 1925 George stopped working. Even after George left, the company kept getting bigger. George traveled, camped, and hunted. Then, he began to have a hard time walking.

George always wore a business suit and dress shoes, even when he was in his own house.

George's doctor told him that he had a sickness in his **spine.** The doctor said the sickness would get worse. George died at home in 1932. He was 78 years old.

George left all of his money to the University of Rochester. He said that the president of the university could live in his house.

Fact File

- When George was young, he made puzzles and toys.

- George did not like being famous. He tried to keep people from knowing much about him. He did not like to have his picture taken.

- George liked to cook so much that he wrote a book of recipes.

- George liked listening to music, so he hired someone to come to his house and play the organ for him every day.

Timeline

1854	George Eastman is born in Waterville, New York.
1862	George's father dies.
1868	George begins his **messenger** job.
1879	George gets a **patent** for machine that coats dry **plates** with **chemicals.**
1881	Eastman Dry Plate Company is started.
1884	George invents roll film.
1888	George's company makes the first handheld box camera.
1892	The name of George's company is changed to Eastman Kodak.
1900	Eastman Kodak introduces the $1 Brownie camera.
1907	George's mother dies.
1925	George retires from Eastman Kodak.
1932	George dies on March 14.

Glossary

advertise   to tell people about a product to try to get them to buy it

boarding house   house where people pay for a room to live in and food to eat

bookkeeper   person who keeps track of money that a company takes in and spends

chemical   special substance that can be mixed with water or other chemicals to make something happen, such as take a picture or do an experiment

dental clinic   place where people can go to have their teeth fixed

experiment   test that is done to discover or prove something

frame   one picture on a roll of film

laboratory   place to do experiments

mansion   large, fancy house

messenger   person who delivers packages and messages

orchard   large number of fruit trees that are planted together

patent   government papers that give an inventor the right to be the only one to make something

photography   art of taking pictures

plate   thick, flat piece of glass used to make a photograph

reel   part of a fishing rod that winds up the fishing line

spine   group of bones in the middle of the back

woodstove   special stove that burns wood and can be used for cooking or to heat a building

More Books to Read

An older reader can help you with these books:

Aller, Susan B. *George Eastman*. Minneapolis: Lerner, 2003.

Czech, Kenneth P. *Snapshot*. Minneapolis: Lerner, 1996.

Pflueger, Linda. *George Eastman: Bringing Photography to the People*. Berkeley Heights, N.J.: Enslow, 2002.

Index